SOUTH-WEST
ENGLAND
from the air

IAN HAY
Text by
GRAHAM PRITCHARD

MYRIAD

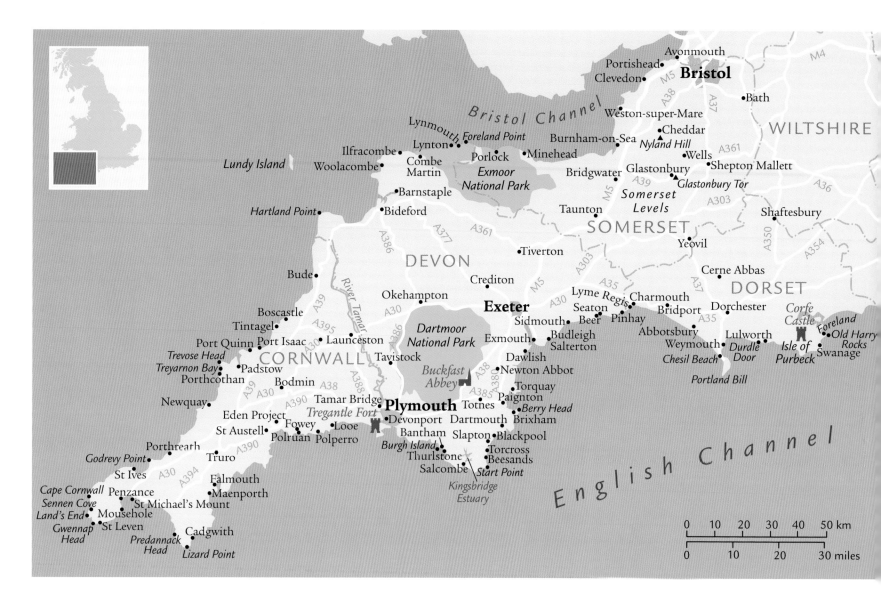

Above right: Combe Martin, North Devon; right: The Circus, Bath; title page: Eden Project, Cornwall

First published in 2009 by Myriad Books Limited
35 Bishopsthorpe Road, London SE26 4PA

Photographs copyright © Ian Hay
Text copyright © Graham Pritchard

Graham Pritchard has asserted his right under the Copyright, Designs and Patents Act 1998 to be
identified as the author of this work.

ISBN 1 84746 267 7
EAN 978 1 84746 267 1

Designed by Jerry Goldie Graphic Design
Printed in China

www.myriadbooks.com

CONTENTS

INTRODUCTION

What do people mean when they refer to south-west England? For some it is Devon and Cornwall, the two counties that form the western "tail" of England. For others the definition includes the counties of Bristol, Somerset and Dorset, and we agree with them. In this book you will find some of the wonders, natural and manmade, that this fascinating region has to offer.

A defining feature of the south-west is its magnificent coastline: of its total 711 miles (1144km), 630 miles (1015km) are accessible to visitors along the South West Coast Path. Britain's longest national trail, it snakes its way along the coast from Minehead in Somerset, through Devon and Cornwall, round to South Haven Point in Dorset. Hardened ramblers can complete the walk in a month; most people tackle it in smaller sections at a gentler pace, revelling in the sights, sounds and fresh air.

With your feet firmly on the ground you get a feel of an idyllic beach, a quaint village or a bustling city. But the fresh perspective of seeing new or well-known places from above can bring insights into how a town or village has developed as it has, or why a beauty spot has remained off the beaten track.

Bath's elegant Georgian crescents and circles are even more striking when seen from the air. The full glory of the architect's original vision springs to life. And from above it becomes clearer why certain parts of Exmoor have remained untamed while others parts are farmed. Sometimes human endeavours result in jarring images such as the Cornish china clay pits at Wheal Martin.

The south-west has always been strategically important for the whole country. The significance of Plymouth (left) was recognised long before Sir Francis Drake insisted on finishing his game of bowls on Plymouth Hoe before setting sail to defeat the Spanish Armada in 1588. From above the nearby Royal Citadel looks threatening and impregnable.

All across the region, nature's power and force are evident. The waves crashing against the rocks at Land's End and Berry Head always inspire wonder as you watch them. Further along the coast in Dorset, nature has worked for thousands of years to carve out the marvel that is Lulworth Cove and create the chalk stacks of Old Harry Rocks.

This is the home of Cornish pasties, Devon cream teas, Dorset knobs and Somerset cider. But seen from the air, there is even more to enjoy.

Graham Pritchard

Left: Plymouth Hoe with the Royal Citadel in the foreground.

BRISTOL & SOMERSET

Bristol has a rich maritime history. In the 15th and 16th centuries, ships left the port loaded with settlers bound for colonies in the New World. By the 18th century, tobacco, sugar, rum and cocoa flooded into the city – all by-products of the burgeoning slave trade. Bristol merchants and sea captains became so rich from the trade that they established fashionable suburbs such as Clifton. Slowly, the docks became less prosperous but Isambard Kingdom Brunel revived the city's fortunes with the building of the Clifton Suspension Bridge and the SS *Great Britain*.

Somerset is famous for its beautiful rolling countryside. The Quantock and Mendip Hills, the low-lying Somerset Levels and the heather-clad uplands of the Exmoor National Park are all well-known beauty spots. Small market towns predominate with two exquisite small cities – Bath and Wells. The coastline is dotted with resorts such as Minehead, Burnham-on-Sea and Weston-Super-Mare.

CITIES OF EMPIRE

The Romans probably occupied *Aquae Sulis* – modern-day Bath (above) – shortly after they invaded Britain in AD43. They were attracted by the natural hot springs, still an important sight for tourists today who visit in their millions. By the 18th century the properties around the green expanse of Queen Square in Bristol (right) were the city's best addresses. After the American Revolution, the former colonies of America established their first embassy here.

BRISTOL

Bristol, on the river Avon, is now England's sixth largest city, and the ninth largest in the UK. From 1155 when it was granted its charter it became an important port. In the 17th century a new trade was established between Africa and the American colonies and Bristol became a centre for the slave trade. To meet the ever-increasing demands, a new harbour, the Floating Harbour, was completed in the city centre in 1809. New docks on the outskirts of the city led to the Floating Harbour becoming redundant towards the end of the 20th century and a prime site for redevelopment. Since the 1980s millions of pounds have been spent on Europe's largest dock regeneration programme. In addition to the Canon's Marsh Amphitheatre on the water's edge (right) Millennium Square boasts the Orange Imaginarium at the new At-Bristol Science Education Centre. Cabot Circus, the new retail and leisure development in the Broadmead area of the city, scooped the Best Shopping Centre of the Year in Europe award in 2008. Away from the hustle and bustle of everyday life, calm can be found in John Wesley's Chapel, the oldest Methodist chapel in the world.

THE NATURAL WORLD AND THE NEW WORLD

Bristol Zoo (below) opened in 1836 and is the world's oldest provincial zoo. Its breeding programme includes a number of firsts: the first chimpanzee born in Europe in 1934 and the first black rhino born in Britain in 1958. In the 1960s the zoo starred in the BBC TV programme *Animal Magic* with Johnny Morris. Cabot Tower (right), on Brandon Hill, was erected in 1897. It commemorates John Cabot who sailed from Bristol 400 years earlier and discovered the land that became Canada. The 105ft (32m) high tower was designed by William Venn Gough and paid for by public subscription.

SS *GREAT BRITAIN*

When she was launched in Bristol in 1843, Isambard Kingdom Brunel's SS *Great Britain* (below) was the largest ship afloat. She was the first ocean-going liner with a screw propeller and an iron hull. After travelling 32 times round the world and more than a million miles, she ended her sailing days in the Falkland Islands in 1886 as a glorified coalbunker. Towed back to her original dry-dock in Bristol in 1970, the SS *Great Britain* underwent major renovation. Since opening to the public in July 2006 the ship has become an award-winning visitor attraction.

CLIFTON AND AVONMOUTH

Isambard Kingdom Brunel was just 24 in 1830 when he was commissioned to build the Clifton Suspension Bridge (above). Its construction was dogged by financial and political problems and Brunel died five years before it was completed in 1864. The bridge spans the Avon Gorge 245ft (76m) above the river and has become a symbol of the city of Bristol. Modern weight restrictions mean that only cars and light trucks can cross the bridge now; nevertheless 4 million vehicles use it every year.

As the name suggests Avonmouth docks (right) lie at the mouth of the river Avon. They are part of the port of Bristol. The first dock, Old Dock, was opened in 1877 and was joined in 1908 by the larger Royal Edward Dock. Today Avonmouth is one of the country's major ports for chilled food, particularly fruit and vegetables. In September 2008, the 46,000-tons *Seven Seas Voyager* docked at Avonmouth, the first of what is hoped will be many cruise ships bringing visitors to Bristol.

PORTISHEAD AND CLEVEDON

Portishead Quays (left) is fast becoming one of the best-equipped marinas in the South-West. The 250-berth marina opened in 2001 in the former Portishead docks. From the navigation light at the end of Battery Point (below centre) you can enjoy fine views of the two Severn Crossings upstream. Sir John Betjeman described Clevedon pier (below) as "the most beautiful pier in England". Opened in 1869, it is 738ft (225m) long and 48ft (14.5m) high. This seaside town, made popular by the Victorians, also boasts the Curzon cinema. It opened in 1912 and claims to be the world's oldest continually-running, purpose-built cinema.

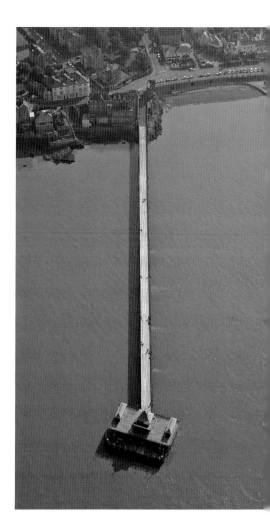

BATH

Bath was founded in Celtic times on the site of naturally occurring hot springs in the valley of the river Avon. By the 2nd century the Romans had built their baths and their *Aquae Sulis* could boast a *calidarium*, a *tepidarium* and a *frigidarium*. After a period of neglect in the intervening centuries, Bath revived during the Elizabethan era as a spa. Queen Elizabeth I made it a city by royal charter in 1590. Alongside the Pump Rooms with their Roman Baths in the city centre (right) stands the majestic Bath Abbey. Completed in 1611, it was the third church to occupy the site. During the 18th century Bath became the fashionable place to "take the waters". Local residents included Thomas Gainsborough, Thomas Lawrence and William Friese-Greene, the father of cinematography. Jane Austen lived in the city with her family between 1801 and 1806. Although Jane never liked the city, she is honoured today with the Jane Austen Centre and a city walk. Bath was declared a World Heritage Site in 1987.

Many of Bath's landmark buildings are the result of a building boom in the 18th century. The Circus (below left) was designed by the architect John Wood the Elder and completed by his son, John Wood the Younger, in 1768.

The Royal Crescent (right) was also the work of the younger man. Completed in 1774, it is Bath's best-known address today. Lansdown Crescent (left), overlooking the rest of the city, was designed by John Palmer and completed in 1793. Robert Adam's Pulteney Bridge over the river (above) is based on Palladio's unused design for the Rialto Bridge in Venice. The bridge dates from 1773 and is one of the few surviving structures in the world that combine a bridge and shopping arcade.

SHEPTON MALLET

Shepton Mallet (right and below) featured as *Sepeton* in the Domesday Book in 1086. Henry I gave it to the Malet family in 1100, and its new name was one of Britain's first double-barrelled place names. In the 19th century brewing joined the town's industries of silk and wool. In 1864 the Anglo-Bavarian brewery was established here, the first maker of lager in the country. The brewery building is still a local landmark, although earmarked for redevelopment. The iconic sparkling pear cider, Babycham, was invented here in the late 1950s. Today the town is home to two international drinks companies, including Europe's largest cider plant which produces Gaymer's Olde English and Blackthorn ciders. Shepton Mallet boasts the country's oldest prison still in use. During the Second World War the buildings were used to store important documents from the Public Record Office in London. They included the Magna Carta, the Domesday Book and the piece of paper signed by Hitler and Neville Chamberlain at the 1939 Munich Conference.

WELLS

Wells (right and below) has been a city since 1205 and is England's smallest. It takes its name from three wells: one in the marketplace and two in the grounds of the cathedral and bishop's palace. The roots of Wells cathedral go back to 909 although the foundations of the Gothic building we see today date from 1180. The then bishop, Bishop Reginald, lived to see the building consecrated, but died before it was granted cathedral status in 1245. The distinctive octagonal Lady Chapel at the east end was completed in 1326. Also of note is the unique Wells clock which dates from 1390: its face shows the Earth at the centre of a pre-Copernican universe. The city was the final setting of the Bloody Assizes after the Monmouth Rebellion in 1685. During the course of one day over 500 people were tried and many were executed. The original definition of Cheddar cheese meant it had to be made within 30 miles (48km) of Wells cathedral.

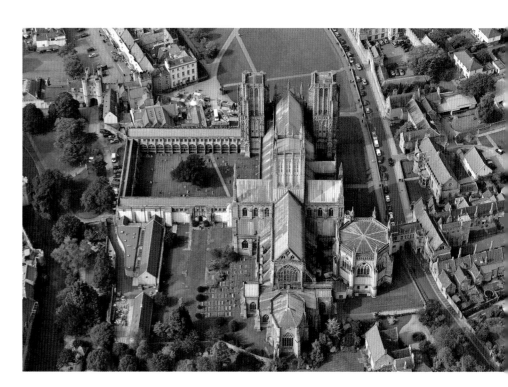

GLASTONBURY

The small town of Glastonbury, said to be the last resting place of King Arthur and the Holy Grail, is steeped in history, legend and myth. Glastonbury Abbey (foreground above) dates from 704 and is considered to be the first Christian sanctuary in Britain: by the Middle Ages it was the richest abbey in the country. When Henry VIII ordered its destruction in 1539, the last abbot was hung, drawn and quartered on Glastonbury Tor for his defiance. Glastonbury festival is the world's longest running greenfield music and performing arts festival. It is held at Worthy Farm, six miles from the town. Entrance to the first festival in 1970 cost £1 and included free fresh milk from the farm. The town of Glastonbury demonstrated its new age credentials, and gained a certain notoriety in 1999, when cannabis plants were found in its public floral displays.

GLASTONBURY TOR

Over the centuries Glastonbury Tor (right and below) has become a place of pilgrimage. The conical tor rises 518ft (158m) from the Somerset Levels. It is topped by the ruins of a 14th century chapel dedicated to St Michael, which was in turn built on the site of an earlier church destroyed by an earthquake in 1275. Archaeological finds indicate that the tor was occupied from the early Middle Ages although mystery still surrounds the purpose of the seven levels of terraces that encircle it. Today the tor is owned and maintained by the National Trust. At the foot of the tor is the Chalice Well natural spring which has been providing water continually for the past 2,000 years. The well became a World Peace Garden in 2001.

YEOVIL

On the old Roman road from Dorchester to the Fosse
Way at Ilchester lies the market town of Yeovil (above). It
featured as the thriving market community of *Givle* in the
Domesday Book, with about 1,000 inhabitants. King John
granted Yeovil its charter in 1205. The Black Death of 1348
and fires in 1499, 1620 and 1643 wrought havoc in the town.
Since 1915 Yeovil has gained a reputation as a centre for
the aircraft and defence industries. Major employers in
the town today are AgustaWestland, manufacturers of
helicopters, Normalair-Garrett, builders of aircraft
oxygen systems, and BAE Systems, producers of military
software. The local football team Yeovil Town FC
currently play in Coca Cola League One. Over the years
they have made a name for themselves as giant-killers,
knocking out much higher teams in the FA Cup
competition.

TAUNTON & BRIDGWATER

The "town on the river Tone", Taunton (above and left) was
important in Saxon times, yet only became the county town
of Somerset in 1366. The Duke of Monmouth crowned
himself king of England here in 1685 and, after the
Monmouth Rebellion, "hanging" Judge Jeffreys held sway at
the Bloody Assizes courts. Taunton's reputation was such
that Queen Victoria would allegedly draw the curtains in
her train while travelling through. The County Cricket
Ground, the country's most south-westerly first-class
ground, has been home to English women's cricket since
2006. By 1500 Bridgwater (right), on the banks of the river
Parrett, was Somerset's largest port, until it was overtaken
by Bristol in the 18th century. Unlike Bristol, Bridgwater
was not involved in the slave trade and was the first place in
the country to petition Parliament to stop the trade in 1797.

THE SOMERSET LEVELS

The Somerset Levels cover 160,000 acres of sparsely populated land between the Quantock and Mendip Hills. About 70% of the land is grassland, the rest arable.

The Battle of Sedgemoor, the last battle on English soil, took place outside the village of Westonzoyland in 1685. It was the final stage of the failed Monmouth Rebellion, when the rebel James Scott, 1st Duke of Monmouth, attempted to claim the throne of James II of England. The

village pub, the Sedgemoor Inn, dates from the time of the battle.

King's Sedgemoor Drain (right), one of the main drainage channels in the Levels, was originally built in 1797-8 to drain the King's Sedge Moor north of the village of Middlezoy (above). The adjacent farmland is now the Greylake RSPB nature reserve and is home to curlews, lapwings, skylarks, snipe and yellow wagtails.

CHEDDAR GORGE

Carved out of the southern slopes of the Mendip Hills above the village of Cheddar, the magnificent Cheddar Gorge (left and right) attracts over half a million visitors a year. It is the largest gorge in the UK, with a maximum depth of 371ft (113m) and the highest inland cliffs in Britain. An almost vertical rocky cliff on the southern side contrasts with a steep grassy slope on the northern side. The B3135 road snakes its way along the bottom of the gorge. In one of the Cheddar Caves, Gough's Cave, Britain's oldest complete human skeleton was discovered in 1903. Known as Cheddar Man, he is reckoned to be 9,000 years old. The caves were possibly used in prehistoric times for cheese-making. Today you can still see cheese being made in the lower gorge at the Cheddar Gorge Cheese Factory.

NYLAND HILL

Nyland Hill (right) rises 250ft (76m) from the low-lying moors to the south of Cheddar. It is surrounded by Cheddar and Draycott moors. From the top fine views are to be had of Cheddar reservoir (left). This almost circular artificial reservoir was built in the 1930s and has a capacity of 1,350 million gallons. It was the first reservoir in Britain to allow sailing on its waters.

WESTON-SUPER-MARE

At the beginning of the 19th century Weston-super-Mare consisted of just 30 houses. With the Victorian era came tourists: Reeves (now known as the Royal Hotel) was the town's first hotel, built in 1808. The railway reached Weston in 1841 and brought day-trippers and holidaymakers in their masses from Bristol, South Wales and the Midlands. Isambard Kingdom Brunel lived in Weston with his family while supervising work on the Bristol and Exeter railway. Birnbeck pier (top of picture, right) is the only pier in the country linking the mainland to an offshore island. The town's first pier, it dates from 1867. Weston's Grand Pier opened in 1906 and is 1,300ft (400m) long. In July 2008 fire destroyed the pier-end pavilion (below). After the fire, a competition to design a new pavilion was won by Angus Meek Architects of Bristol. The new Grand Pier Pavilion with its glass front and sweeping lines is due to open by 2010. The Weston miniature railway is a popular attraction on Marine Parade. Paddle steamers still offer pleasure trips up and down the Bristol Channel from Knightstone Island (lower picture), which has been revived with luxury apartments and shops.

BURNHAM-ON-SEA

The holiday resort of Burnham-on-Sea (above) is noted for its beach and mudflats, which are characteristic of Bridgwater Bay and the Bristol Channel. Second only in its tidal range to eastern Canada's Bay of Fundy, the Bristol Channel tide can sometimes recede one and a half miles. Burnham's concrete pier (right) was built in 1914 to replace an earlier stone pier. It claims to be the shortest pier in Britain, if not the world! Of the town's two lighthouses, the Round Tower lighthouse, dating from 1829, is now a private house rented out as holiday accommodation. The aptly named "lighthouse on legs" sits on stilts on the foreshore. It was built in 1832 and is still used as a navigation aid for shipping.

MINEHEAD

The popular seaside resort of Minehead, overlooked by North Hill, nestles between Exmoor and the sea. It has been attracting holidaymakers since the mid 19th century. The white roofs (foreground) belong to the Skyline pavilion at the Butlins holiday resort, which opened in 1965. Minehead is at one end of the South West Coast Path, which stretches 630 miles (1014km) round the coast of Devon and Cornwall to Poole in Dorset. In the other direction, the West Somerset Railway, Britain's longest heritage railway, heads out through unspoilt countryside skirting the Quantock Hills to Bishops Lydeard near Taunton.

PORLOCK

The mile-long shingle beach at Porlock (left) is backed by salt marshes and the rolling hills of Exmoor. At its eastern end rises the rocky outcrop of Hurlstone Point. In winter, the area attracts wildfowl and waders such as spoonbills, ospreys and snow buntings. The village of Porlock appeared as *Portloc* in the Domesday Book. Over the years this tranquil village has attracted poets such as Wordsworth and Coleridge, who is commemorated by the Coleridge Way footpath. To the south of Porlock, the picturesque Hawkcombe valley (above) extends to Hawkcombe Head on Exmoor and is typical of the wooded valleys on the moor.

EXMOOR

Wild, rugged and breathtakingly beautiful, Exmoor consists of 267 square miles of hilly open heath and moorland. Designated a national park in 1954, 72% of its area lies in Somerset, the rest in Devon. For over 3,000 years sheep have grazed on the moor which is also home to the Exmoor pony, the oldest of the native British ponies. During Charles I's reign, Exmoor became a royal forest and hunting ground. At Dillacombe (above) remnants of old enclosures can be seen, an attempt to tame the moor for agriculture. Landacre bridge (right) over the river Barle is the oldest arched bridge on Exmoor.

SIMONSBATH

The valley of the river Barle to the south of Simonsbath (right) is considered by many to be the real Exmoor. James Boevey, at one time the warden of the royal forest and hunting ground, built himself a house in Simonsbath in the mid-17th century and for 150 years this was the only dwelling on the moor. The house is now the Simonsbath House Hotel, conveniently situated on the Two Moors Way footpath linking Dartmoor with Exmoor.

NORTH DEVON

The birthplace of a saint, the UK's oldest borough, the country's best beach and the starting point for one of the toughest challenges for youngsters are all to be found in north Devon. The north Devon coastline is one of the most rugged and most dramatic in England; it is also the highest in England. Tucked away along the coast are sheltered coves offering a safe haven for shipping, while the west-facing sandy beaches are the favourite haunts of swimmers and surfers. The wilds of Exmoor contrast with the more gentle countryside along the meandering valleys of the rivers Taw and Torridge. Historic towns and picturesque villages complete the picture and are the reason that visitors return year after year.

WILD AND WINDSWEPT

As the clouds clear over Lundy Island (above) the granite mass of this windswept island is revealed in all its glory. The small resident population of 28 is hugely outnumbered by large colonies of seabirds that nest on the island. The vast expanse of beach at Saunton Sands (right) extends for three miles (5km). Behind lies the UNESCO designated Biosphere Reserve of Braunton Burrows, a large area of dunes and marshes.

FORELAND POINT

The rocky headland of Foreland Point (above) is the most northerly point on the Devon coast. It is also the most northerly point of the Exmoor National Park and separates Lynmouth Bay from Countisbury Cove. The highest cliff rises 292ft (89m) above the high water line, but the highest point of the whole headland, at 991ft (302m), is further inland near the tiny village of Countisbury. The Exmoor Heritage Coast extends to the east and west of Foreland Point and is England's highest coastline. Located 220ft (67m) above the high tide sits the Lynmouth Foreland lighthouse (below). Established in 1900, the lighthouse was automated in 1994 and is now controlled by the Trinity House Operations Control Centre in Essex.

LYNTON AND LYNMOUTH

The pretty harbour village of Lynmouth (below) sits at the confluence of the East and West Lynn rivers and is sheltered by Foreland Point. The wooded hillsides, narrow valleys and gushing rivers led the Victorians to call this part of the coast "little Switzerland". Thomas Gainsborough spent his honeymoon in Lynmouth and described it as "the most beautiful place for a landscape painter this country can boast". Disaster struck Lynmouth on 15 and 16 August 1952. After nine inches of rain, a raging torrent raced through the village, causing heavy damage and the loss of 34 lives. The village was rebuilt after the flooding and the river diverted around the village. Five hundred feet (152m) above Lynmouth is its sister village of Lynton (left and below centre), a popular holiday destination in Victorian times. In order to ease visitors' journeys up the cliff from the harbour an ingenious cliff railway was opened in 1890. The Lynton and Lynmouth cliff railway still operates today between Valentine's Day and the beginning of November.

COMBE MARTIN AND ILFRACOMBE

Set on the western edge of Exmoor, Combe Martin (below) boasts the longest main road of any village in England. It runs through the village along the valley of the river Umber for over two miles (3km). Taking pride of place are the 13th century St Peter ad Vincular church and the 17th century Pack of Cards inn, which was built by George Ley of Marwood in celebration of a large win at cards. Today at the Combe Martin Wildlife & Dinosaur Park visitors can see the country's first animatronic Tyrannosaurus Rex. Further west along the coast lies Ilfracombe (right), which featured as *Alfreinscoma* in the Exeter Domesday Book of 1086. This colourful holiday resort with its floral displays has frequently won the Britain in Bloom competition. Its harbour, the largest on the north Devon coast, is protected from the east by Hillsborough Hill which is 447ft (136m) high. Ilfracombe's oldest building, St Nicholas' Chapel, sits on the smaller Lantern Hill, which protects the harbour from the Bristol Channel. The architecturally striking Landmark Theatre overlooking the seafront opened in 1998 and is still a source of controversy. Between March and October you can take the ferry between Ilfracombe and Lundy Island.

WOOLACOMBE VILLAGE BEACH AND BARNSTAPLE

The sandy beach at Woolacombe (above) extends two and a quarter miles (3.5km) along Morte Bay between Baggy and Morte Points. This Blue Flag beach has long been a favourite with surfers and has been voted one of the best beaches in the country. During the Second World War Woolacombe was home to the US Army Training Centre. Troops practised here for the D-Day landings as the long beach closely resembled the landing area at Omaha Beach in Normandy.

Barnstaple (right), on the banks of the river Taw, claims to be the UK's oldest borough. It has been the major market in the area since Saxon times, and the Domesday Book records that it had a mint. By the Middle Ages Barnstaple had become an important trading centre for wool. The town's status as a market centre was further enhanced in 1855 with the building of

Butchers Row and Pannier Market. Today some of the 33 shops in Butchers Row still trade as butchers, while others sell local produce. The Pannier Market is still held three times a week and it has been rated as one of the best food markets in the country.

Traffic congestion in Barnstaple was finally eased in May 2007 with the opening of the western bypass. The five spans of the quarter-mile long (409m) Downstream Bridge carry traffic over the river Taw away from the town centre.

TIVERTON

Tiverton's roots go back to the Stone Age. Its name is derived from *Twyverton*, meaning the town on two fords – in this case on the rivers Lowman and Exe. Tiverton castle was built on the orders of Henry 1 in 1106 and in the Middle Ages it was home to the powerful Earls of Devon. In the 16th and 17th centuries Tiverton prospered due to the wool trade, but declined during the Industrial Revolution. By the 1850s Tiverton was on the way up again, with a new lace industry and the arrival of a branch of the Great Western canal (above centre). From 1835 till 1865 Lord Palmerston was the MP for Tiverton. Renowned for his interventionist "gunboat diplomacy", Palmerston served as Foreign Secretary for some 20 years followed by two periods as Prime Minister when Queen Victoria's empire was at its peak. Tiverton kept its own independent police force until 1945.

OKEHAMPTON

Like so many towns in the region, Okehampton's prosperity is based on the wool trade. On the northern edge of Dartmoor, the town lies on the banks of the river Okement, from where it gets its name. Okehampton Castle was the only castle to be listed in the Domesday Book. Its keep was extended by the 1st Earl of Devon, Sir Robert de Courtenay, in the 14th century but only ruins remain. Today Okehampton (left) is known for its broad main street, Fore Street (below), and its original Victorian shopping arcade with small shops and tearooms. Outside the town, Okehampton camp on Dartmoor is a major army-training base. Every May hundreds of youngsters set off from here on the Ten Tors Challenge.

CREDITON

Crediton (left) in the vale of the river Creedy is known as the birthplace of St Boniface, the patron saint of Germany and Holland, in about 672. The Diocese of Crediton was created in 909 with Edwulf as the first bishop here to cover Devon and Cornwall. The seat was transferred to Exeter in 1050. The cathedral may have occupied the site of what is now Crediton parish church formally known as "the Church of the Holy Cross and the Mother of Him who hung thereon". Today the suffragan Bishop of Crediton assists the diocesan Bishop of Exeter. The pioneering engineer Isambard Kingdom Brunel designed Crediton's station, which is served by two railway lines. The Tarka Line from Exeter through Crediton to Barnstaple follows the rivers Yeo and Taw. The Dartmoor Railway, a heritage line, runs services to Okehampton and is now owned by British American Railway Services.

LUNDY ISLAND

This mainly granite island, rich in fauna and flora, is 12 miles (19km) off the coast, about one third of the way across the Bristol Channel between north Devon and Pembrokeshire. The name Lundy may come from the Norse for puffin, and there is a small colony of puffins on the island today. The island has a very chequered history: times of turmoil when it was run by pirates and privateers contrasted with times of peace when it was owned by private families. In the late 19th century Lundy's rector was Thomas Heaven, and some people referred to the island as the Kingdom of Heaven. Today the National Trust owns Lundy Island, and just 28 people live there. The Landmark Trust manages 23 holiday properties there and owns the main means of transport to the island, the MS *Oldenburg*. Most of the accommodation is located in the south of the island and ranges from a 13th century castle to an old lighthouse and a Georgian-style villa. Lundy features as a sea area in the UK shipping forecast. Two lighthouses warn shipping of the island's 20 miles (32km) of dangerous coastline and adjacent rocks: Lundy North and Lundy South, which both date from 1897.

Above left: the majestic glory of Lundy Island.
Above right: St Helena's church and the Georgian-style Millcombe House surrounded by trees.
Far left: Lundy North lighthouse with the Hen and Chickens rocks in the foreground.
Left: Jenny's Cove with Pyramid Rock on Lundy's west coast.
Right: Beacon Hill, the highest point on the island.

CORNWALL

Cornwall – or Kernow in Cornish – is England's most south-western county and has the best climate too. But the superlatives don't stop there. It is the county with the longest coastline in the UK: 433 miles (697km), including 146 miles (235km) of Heritage coast. It also has some of the best beaches – over 300 – so it is no surprise that Cornwall attracts five million visitors every year, most coming from within the UK. They come to explore the county's natural beauty which dates from the dawn of time, for the pleasure of the seaside resorts and to be inspired by 21st century design. Cornwall has its own history, food and language, which is being actively promoted. According to local folklore the devil never ventured into Cornwall for fear of ending up in a pasty!

SURF AND SAFE ANCHORAGE

Surfers enjoy the thrills and spills of the waves at Newquay (above) which has become the United Kingdom's prime surfing location. The town's Fistral beach has been staging national and international surfing competitions for over 20 years. The more sheltered south coast of Cornwall is characterised by wide estuaries offering safe anchorage. Looe (right) is a popular port of call for holidaymakers, yachtsmen and fans of shark fishing.

BUDE

Bude stands at the mouth of the river Neet on Cornwall's north coast. The name comes from Bede Haven, meaning harbour of holy men. The town's fortunes changed with the opening of the Bude canal (right) in the 1820s. The canal was first mooted in 1774 to link the Bristol and English Channels via the river Tamar, but in the end only 35½ miles (57km) were completed. Its main purpose was agricultural: to transport lime-rich sand to the hinterland where it was used to improve the quality of the soil.

CROOKLETS BEACH, BUDE

Bude developed as a tourist resort with the arrival of the railway in 1898 and the opening of the branch line from Holsworthy – a subsequent casualty of the Beeching cuts in 1966. Visitors were drawn to the area by the fresh Atlantic air and the wide-open scenery.

In the 1950s surfers discovered the delights of Bude's Crooklets beach (below). The broad, west-facing expanse of sand of this Blue Flag beach runs from Wrangles Rock to the north and Barrel Rock in the south. The variety of the waves caters for surfers of all levels. The Bude Surf Club was a founder member in 1955 of the Surf Life Saving Association of Great Britain. A more recent event in Bude has become known locally as "the Bude Boom". At about 11.50 on 26 October 2006 there was a loud and unexplained noise over the town, parts of which experienced property damage. Subsequent suggestions of a possible cause include an RAF aircraft breaking the sound barrier or a meteor exploding out in the atmosphere.

BOSCASTLE

The village of Boscastle (above) grew up around its medieval harbour and clings to the slopes of the valley where the rivers Valency and Jordan meet. The name is derived from now ruined Bottreaux Castle, built in Norman times by the Botterel family. Protected by Pennally Point, Boscastle offers the only natural harbour on this stretch of coast. The two harbour walls were built in 1584 by Sir Richard Grenville. The harbour and much of the surrounding area are now owned by the National Trust. In the afternoon of 16 August 2004 disaster struck Boscastle. After a period of very heavy rain, a flash flood estimated at about 440 million gallons of water raged through the village. Luckily no lives were lost but there was extensive damage. The local council, the National Trust and English Heritage have been at pains to maintain the character of the village during the restoration work. One of Boscastle's most popular attractions is the Museum of Witchcraft, which houses one of the world's most extensive collections of witchcraft-related items. Established in 1960, the museum is open daily from Easter to Halloween.

TINTAGEL HEAD

Tintagel Head (above and left) is one of
Cornwall's most iconic sights. Here stand the
ruins of Tintagel Castle, the legendary
birthplace of King Arthur and home of the
wizard Merlin.

There have been fortifications on this spot
since the Iron Age, but the ruins we see today
date from the 13th century, when the castle
was home to the Earls of Cornwall. At low
tide it is possible to walk through Merlin's
cave, once the favourite hiding place of
smugglers. Tintagel's Old Post Office is a 14th
century stone house, used as a district post
office for 50 years in the 19th century. It is
now owned by the National Trust. At St Paul's
church is the unique and poignant
Miscarriage and Infant Loss Memorial Book,
where parents can record the loss of a baby
from conception to three years old.

SEVEN BAYS FOR SEVEN DAYS

To the west of the Camel estuary and Padstow Bay lies the coastline sometimes described as "seven bays for seven days", punctuated by the headland of Trevose Head. Just visible above the caravan park in the bottom of the picture above is Polverton or Mother Ivey's Bay, then the broad sweep of Harlyn Bay and, beyond, Trevone Bay protected by the cliffs of Gunver Head.

PORT ISAAC

The narrow winding streets of the fishing village of Port Isaac (right) all lead down to its pretty harbour, through which slate, coal, wood and pottery once passed. The village dates from the Middle Ages. With its slate-fronted houses and whitewashed cottages, it is a favourite with film and television programme-makers. The film *Oscar and Lucinda* was shot here as was the ITV series *Doc Martin* starring Martin Clunes.

THE CAMEL ESTUARY

The estuary of the river Camel stretches about five miles (8km) from the coast inland to Wadebridge. The river's name is said to come from the Cornish word for "crooked one". On the western shore sits the town of Padstow. It was once considered the ecclesiastical capital of Cornwall because of the nearby monastery founded by St Petroc, who came from Ireland in the 6th century.

Today Padstow is a bustling fishing port and holiday resort, made famous by the restaurateur Rick Stein. From Padstow you can take the Black Tor ferry to the village opposite. Rock (shown above) is home to more millionaires than anywhere else in Cornwall. It attracts rich and famous visitors, and has been dubbed the Kensington of Cornwall and Britain's Saint-Tropez.

PORTHCOTHAN

Popular with surfers, the village of Porthcothan (right) is set around a pretty sandy beach crossed by a small stream. The cliffs and area to the north of the bay are owned by the National Trust and are home to a wide variety of flora and fauna.

TREVOSE HEAD

The lighthouse at Trevose Head (above) sits on granite cliffs that tower 150ft (46m) over the sea. A lighthouse was first proposed for this spot in 1809 but it only became operational in 1847, and was automated in 1995. It is open to the public on weekdays. The new Trevose Head lifeboat station and slipway (left) opened in August 2006 and houses the Padstow lifeboat.

TREYARNON AND CONSTANTINE BAYS

South of Trevose Head lie two more of the "seven bays for seven days". The long stretch of Constantine Bay (left, foreground) is separated from Trevose golf course by sand dunes topped with marram grass. Top quality waves make Constantine Bay a favourite with surfers. The smaller Treyarnon Bay (left, centre) is set in an area of outstanding natural beauty with rock pools and idyllic small coves. To the south of the bay, erosion has produced a series of deep coves (see inset). Running right to left are Fox Cove, Warren Cove and Pepper Cove. Trethias Island separated by a narrow channel, guards the entrance to Treyarnon Bay, and is home to nesting seabirds.

49

NEWQUAY

Newquay grew up around its fishing harbour which thrived on the humble pilchard until the industry's demise early in the 20th century. The beaches stretching round Newquay Bay became the main attraction for visitors and turned the area into a major holiday destination. The local population of 20,000 swells to 100,000 during the summer months. In recent years surfers of all levels have flocked to Newquay, which proudly claims to be the surfing capital of Britain. Beginners head to the Great Western beach with its smaller surf, while experienced surfers head across the fairways of Newquay golf course to the more exposed Fistral beach with its rolling Atlantic breakers. Rated one of the best surfing beaches in the UK, Fistral beach has hosted many national and international surfing competitions. In 2010 it will host the main events in Rescue 2010, the life-saving world championships. Overlooking Fistral beach with fine views of Towan Head is the Headland Hotel, which has been welcoming visitors including royalty since 1900.

PORTREATH

The village of Portreath (above) was once a busy port, and the present harbour dates from 1760. Ships laden with copper ore would sail over to Swansea in south Wales and return with coal. The first tramway in Cornwall was built in 1809 to bring the copper ore to Portreath from further afield. Now pleasurecraft and fishing boats occupy the harbour and the tramway is a footpath enjoyed by walkers and cyclists.

GODREVY POINT

Godrevy Point (left) marks the northern limit of St Ives Bay and is owned by the National Trust. The lighthouse on Godrevy Island was erected in 1859 and features in Virginia Woolf's novel *To the Lighthouse*.

ST IVES

The roots of St Ives (right) can be traced back to St Ia who, in the 6th century, is reputed to have sailed over from Ireland on a leaf! St Ives received its royal charter in 1295. Sheltered by St Ives Head, this thriving holiday resort was voted "seaside town of the year" by the Guardian in 2007.

ST IVES

Fishing and mining were both important to the growth of St Ives. The Downalong area around the harbour was home to fishing families while, higher up, the Upalong district housed mining families. In 1877 the railway reached the town with the opening of the branch line from St Erth at the head of the Hayle estuary. This put St Ives firmly on the map and much of the present town was built towards the end of the 19th century to cater for the increasing number of visitors. The railway line is now a tourist attraction in its own right, and is considered to be one of England's most picturesque lines. Today sun-worshippers flock to the town's several beaches with surfers making for the breakers on Porthmeor beach (above).

ARTISTS' COLONY, ST IVES

Artists have always been drawn to St Ives by the quality of its light. Early visitors included Sydney Lawrence, Walter Sickert, James Whistler and JMW Turner. The artists' colony of today was founded in 1928 by the Cornish artist Alfred Wallis and his friends Ben Nicholson and Christopher Wood. In 1939 Ben Nicholson and Barbara Hepworth settled in St Ives, along with Naum Gabo, and during the next 15 years St Ives celebrated its golden age.

Art galleries abound in the town and in 1993 the second branch of the Tate gallery outside London opened. The Tate also looks after the nearby Barbara Hepworth museum and sculpture garden. The annual St Ives September festival of art and music is one of the longest running in Britain.

LONG CARN WHIRLPOOL

The sea crashes on the rocks below the cliffs between the isolated Porthmoina and Portheras coves (above) forming a whirlpool. Above, the area is rich in Cornish history: close to the path at Trevowhan cliff there are open mine shafts; a little distance inland is the megalithic Boskednan stone circle, also known as the Nine Maidens, which may once have had as many as 22 upright stones.

PENDEEN TIN

Tin has been mined around Pendeen since the beginning of the 18th century. The Geevor mine (left) was one of the last to open; the Levant mine nearby is one of Cornwall's most famous. After production ceased in 1990, the old mine buildings were adapted and the Geevor Tin Mine Heritage Centre opened in August 1993. The centre, where visitors can learn about the mining and processing of tin, is now the largest preserved mining centre in Britain.

CAPE CORNWALL

To the west of the village of St Just lies Cape Cornwall (above). One of only two capes in Britain – the other is Cape Wrath in Scotland – Cape Cornwall is where the waters of the English Channel meet those of St George's Channel. The cape affords fine views of Land's End to the south. Cape Cornwall School is the most westerly school in Britain and Cornwall's smallest secondary school.

SENNEN COVE

Protected by the Pedn-men-du headland, Sennen Cove (left) lies snugly in the south-east corner of Whitesand Bay. The wide sandy beach is popular with swimmers and surfers alike. Between 2005 and 2007 the beach boasted the UK's first-ever canine lifeguard, a seven-year-old Newfoundland dog called Bilbo. Further out to sea you can sometimes catch sight of basking sharks (right). Together with dolphins, porpoises and grey seals they are attracted to the area by the clear, clean water and abundant supply of food.

LAND'S END

The most westerly point in mainland Britain, Land's End (right and below), is still an awe-inspiring sight if somewhat commercialised. The famous signpost showing the distances to New York and John O'Groats is now part of a theme park. Among the visitors are the End-to-Enders, who turn straight round and set off on the 874 mile (1407km) journey to the northernmost point, John O'Groats in Scotland. In 1879 Cornishman Robert Carlyle was the first person to achieve this feat – pushing a wheelbarrow. One and a half miles (2.4km) offshore, the Longships Lighthouse (above) stands guard on Carn Bras, the largest of the Longships Rocks.

PORDENNACK POINT

Heading south from Land's End, the beaches of the north Cornish coast give way to a more rugged coastline. In the foreground of the picture above, just offshore, sits the island of Enys Dodnan, famed for its arched rock. Behind lie the headlands of Pordennack Point, Carn Boel and beyond Mill Bay, Carn Les Boel. Walkers on this stretch of the South West Coast Path are often rewarded by sightings of seabirds including gannets, guillemots and razorbills.

MOUSEHOLE

One of the most picturesque villages in the whole of Cornwall, Mousehole (pronounced "Mowzel") is set around its harbour (right). Many of the houses are built of the local Lamorna granite. Near the harbour a plaque marks the house of Dolly Pentreath, who was reputed to have been the last person to speak only Cornish. She died in 1777. In 1937, Dylan Thomas spent his honeymoon in Mousehole with his wife Caitlin. History does not relate if they ate stargazy pie, the local speciality which has fish heads sticking out through the piecrust.

PORTHCHAPEL BEACH

Porthchapel beach (below) is protected by the cliffs of Pedn-men-an-mere, which is a Cornish name meaning rocky headland by the sea. Close by is the Minack theatre, where visitors have been enjoying the works of Shakespeare and Gilbert & Sullivan in the open air since 1932.

GWENNAP HEAD

The South West Coast Path is clearly visible as it traces its way across Gwennap Head (above), the most southerly point of the Penwith peninsula. This section is also known as the Penwith Heritage Coast which stretches 33 miles (53km) from St Ives, past Land's End, ending just south of Penzance. An area of outstanding natural beauty, this stretch of the Cornish coast is a favourite with birdwatchers who come to view marine birds such as skuas, whimbrels, petrels and shearwaters. Gwennap Head also attracts rock climbers who relish the challenge of scaling the granite cliff faces, including the well-known Chair Ladder crag.

PENZANCE

Penzance enjoys a sheltered
position on Mount's Bay and a
warmer climate than anywhere else
in Britain. For many years it was
overshadowed by nearby Marazion,
which was mentioned in the
Domesday Book in 1088. Marazion
is the oldest chartered town in
Britain. But Penzance's fortunes
changed: Henry IV granted the
town a royal market, Henry VIII
allowed it to charge harbour dues
and James I made it a borough.
Today Penzance has ship repair and
dry dock facilities, and its harbour
caters for fishing boats and leisure
craft. The Isles of Scilly Steamship
Company runs a seasonal service
between Penzance and the largest
of the islands, St Mary's.

ST MICHAEL'S MOUNT

The Cornish cousin of Mont St-
Michel in France, St Michael's
Mount is linked to Marazion by a
causeway that is passable only at
mid and low tides. The castle and
gardens, home of the St Aubyn
family, are maintained by the
National Trust.

PREDANNACK HEAD

Above the cliffs at Predannack Head (above) lie a
nature reserve and an old airfield opened in 1941.
During the Second World War the RAF flew anti-
submarine missions from Predannack airfield
over the Bay of Biscay. The airfield is now used by
the Royal Navy as a back-up when RNAS Culdrose
gets too busy. It is also the base for the Royal Navy
School of Fire Fighting and an RAF gliding school.
The Lizard national nature reserve covers more
than 4,000 acres, has 18 rare plant species and
nesting sites for ravens and peregrines.

CADGWITH

The pretty fishing village of Cadgwith (right) was
first settled in the Middle Ages. Its two beaches
are divided by a promontory called the Todden.
Big Beach, where fishermen still ply their trade is
the larger; it is also known as the Cove or Fishing
Beach. Swimmers favour the smaller Little Beach
or Little Cove. Until the 1950s pilchard fishing was
very important and in 1904 a record catch of
1,789,000 pilchards was landed over a four-day
period.

LIZARD POINT LIGHTHOUSE

The massed ships of the Spanish Armada were first sighted in 1588 from Lizard Point, the southernmost point in Britain (right). A lighthouse has warned passing ships of the Point's dangerous rocks since 1751. In the foreground are the slipway and the old lifeboat station; the lifeboat station was relocated to Kilcobben Cove on the opposite side of Lizard Point in 1961.

MAENPORTH AND PENDENNIS POINT

Overlooking Falmouth Bay is the small town of Maenporth (above). Its gently shelving, sheltered beach is popular with families with young children. At low tide it is possible to see the wreck of the *Ben Asdale*, a freezer trawler that foundered in extreme weather on 30 December 1978 with the loss of three lives.

Pendennis Castle (below) was built by Henry VIII in 1545, as he feared an attack from the French and Spanish because of his divorce from his first wife, Catherine of Aragon. The castle escaped then because there was no invasion, but it was besieged by Parliamentary forces during the English Civil War in 1646.

ST MAWES

St Mawes (right), at the end of the Roseland peninsula, is named after the Celtic saint Maudez. The sheltered harbour at the entrance of the river Percuil and good beaches nearby make this a popular destination with sailors and holidaymakers. There are ferry services across to St Anthony Head and to Falmouth. The surrounding coastline featured in the television series *Poldark* and Agatha Christie's classic *Murder Ahoy* was filmed in St Mawes. To the west of the town, St Mawes Castle was built at the same time as Pendennis Castle, and both are now in the care of English Heritage.

FALMOUTH

When Sir Walter Raleigh visited Sir John Killigrew at Arwenack House in 1600, there was just a small hamlet where Falmouth stands today. Its geographical situation so impressed him that he advocated the site's development as a port. Falmouth harbour, along with the stretch of water called Carrick Roads, is the deepest natural harbour in western Europe and the third deepest in the world.

Falmouth received its royal charter in 1661. From 1688, for more than 150 years, the town served as the Royal Mail packet station, through which every single piece of mail passed to and from Britain's burgeoning empire. News of Nelson's victory at Trafalgar, and of his death, was received through Falmouth's Fishstrand Quay in 1805. The arrival of the railway in 1863 brought further prosperity to Falmouth. Today's visitors come to enjoy the town's many gardens and sandy beaches, including Gyllyingvase beach (foreground). Falmouth docks (above) were developed from 1858 onwards. They now cover 74 acres with ship repair and dry dock facilities, fish landing and processing and oil storage facilities. Also on the waterfront is the National Maritime Museum Cornwall, a joint project created in 1992 between the National Maritime Museum Greenwich and the former Cornwall Maritime Museum.

Toad, Ratty and Mole, the characters in Kenneth Grahame's book *The Wind in the Willows*, began life in a series of letters Kenneth Grahame wrote to his son in 1907 while staying in Falmouth's Greenbank Hotel.

ST AUSTELL

Cornwall's largest town, St Austell was first mentioned in an account of a visit by Henry VIII. The town's prosperity was based on tin, copper and later china clay. Today visitors come to enjoy the beaches and the Eden Project and the Lost Gardens of Heligan nearby. The St Austell Viaduct (right), to the west of the town, carries the main London to Penzance railway line over the Trenance valley. It is 720ft (219m) long, 115ft (35m) high and dates from 1898. The building in the town centre (far right) is known as the Red Bank; it is now a branch of the NatWest bank. It was built by local architect Silvanus Trevail in 1898 using striking red bricks from Ruabon in north Wales.

WHEAL
MARTYN *overleaf*

North-west of St Austell lie
the two 19th century china
clay pits of Wheal Martyn
and Gomm. Today this 26-
acre site forms the China
Clay Country Park where,
in interactive displays,
visitors can learn about
Cornish china clay's long
history since William
Cookworthy first
discovered it in 1746.

EDEN PROJECT

Since opening in 2001, more than eight million people
have visited the Eden Project, generating some £800
million for the regional economy. The brainchild of Tim
Smit, this environmental project is situated in a disused
china clay pit three miles (5km) to the north-east of St
Austell. During construction of this global garden some
800,000m³ of soil had to be repositioned on the site.
Visitors can see coffee, bamboo and fruiting banana trees
in the tropical Rainforest biome, which is the world's
largest greenhouse – 3.9 acres in area. Grapes and olives
thrive in the smaller, more temperate Mediterranean
biome and in the outdoor biome lavender, tea, hemp and
hops grow. The Core, a new educational centre with
classrooms and exhibition space, opened in 2005. In 2007
the British Construction Industry acclaimed the Eden
Project as the best British building of the past 20 years.

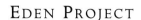

FOWEY

At the head of its estuary, the town of Fowey (above) has long flourished as a port. Overlooking its busy harbour and quaint cottages is Place House, a fortified manor house and home of the Treffry family since the 13th century. Opposite sits the parish church dedicated to St Finn Barr, the first Bishop of Cork. The church tower dates from 1460 and is the second highest in Cornwall. Every year in May, Fowey hosts the Daphne du Maurier festival of art and literature.

POLRUAN

Enjoying a sheltered position away from the prevailing winds, at the entrance to the Fowey estuary, Polruan was once a busy shipbuilding port. The stretches of water known as Polruan Pool and nearby Pont Pill (above) are today favourite moorings for leisure craft. Polruan "castle" is a rectangular blockhouse (foreground left) dating from the end of the 14th century. This was linked by a chain to another blockhouse on the opposite bank of the estuary, and the chain could be raised to protect the harbour from the French or from pirates. The rocks to the seaward side of the Polruan blockhouse are known locally as the Washing Rocks (left).

A short distance upstream from Polruan is the attractive small village of Bodinnick. Right by the water's edge is Ferryside, the du Maurier family home since 1927. It was here in 1928-9 that the author Daphne du Maurier wrote her first book *The Loving Spirit*, first published in 1931. The house is today occupied by Daphne du Maurier's son and his family.

POLPERRO, LOOE AND TREGANTLE FORT

The village of Polperro (left) is one of the most popular in Cornwall, and one of the prettiest. It dates from the 13th century and its charming cottages line the steep-sided valley of the river Pol. Today tourism has replaced fishing as the main industry, but in the 18th century the smuggling of goods over from Guernsey was the favourite occupation. Visitors can learn about both at the unique Museum of Smuggling and Fishing. The seven-arched bridge which carries the A387 over the river Looe dates from 1853. It links East and West Looe (above). Fishing is still an important industry here and the fishing fleet is Cornwall's second largest. Looe is also the home of the Shark Angling Club of Great Britain. The long Banjo pier protects the popular East Looe beach from the river. Looe is considered one of the 10 best places to celebrate the New Year in Britain.

Six-sided but not symmetrical, Tregantle fort (right) dates from 1865. It is situated between Whitsand Bay and the Lynher estuary. The fort's most famous resident was probably Joe Lewis, the American heavyweight boxing champion, who was stationed here during the Second World War.

SOUTH DEVON

The granite landmass of the Dartmoor National Park dominates South Devon. Either side of the rugged and challenging countryside of the moor are the region's two most vibrant and historic cities, Plymouth and Exeter. In between lie fascinating towns and villages. Elegant holiday resorts line the spectacular coastline, nicknamed the English Riviera. Deep estuaries vie with modern multi-berth marinas to offer shelter to the sailor and yachtsman. The railway buff will not be disappointed either with some of the best heritage railways in the country. So step back in time and enjoy life at a slower pace. But life doesn't stand still in south Devon: recently opened attractions include the National Marine Aquarium at Plymouth and Living Coasts at Torquay, Britain's only coastal zoo.

HOME OF THE SENIOR SERVICE

South Devon has a long connection with the Royal Navy, from Drake, Gilbert and Raleigh to the present day. Cadets have been reporting to Dartmouth for officer training since 1863, long before the completion of the Royal Naval College (above) in 1905. On the eastern banks of the river Tamar, the naval facility at Devonport (right) dates back to 1691. Today it is one of the navy's three UK operating bases. In the background rise the bleak hills of Dartmoor.

TAMAR RIVER AND DEVONPORT

From shortly after its source at East Youlstone, four miles (6km) from the north Cornish coast, the river Tamar forms most of the border between the counties of Cornwall and Devon. The most spectacular of the 20 road bridges over the river is the Tamar Bridge (right in above picture). When it opened in 1961, its central span of 1100 feet (335m) made it the UK's longest suspension bridge. Vehicles pay a toll only when leaving Cornwall. To the seaward side of the road bridge, Isambard Kingdom Brunel's Royal Albert Bridge carries the Cornish main railway line from Saltash over to Plymouth. The bridge was opened by Prince Albert in 1859, the year of Brunel's death. The naval dockyards (below) were established on the orders of King William III in 1691. The original name of Plymouth Dock was changed to Devonport in 1823 at the request of local residents.

The four miles (6km) of waterfront, five basins, 14 dry docks and 25 tidal berths of the Royal Naval Dockyard (left) cover 650 acres. Her Majesty's Naval Base Devonport is the largest in Western Europe. The Devonport flotilla (all stationed here) includes 11 frigates, seven Trafalgar class nuclear submarines and the navy's largest ship, HMS *Ocean* (pictured right, prior to sea trials in September 2008 after a major refit). Every two years the public can visit ships and submarines in the dockyards on Navy Day, the Royal Navy's biggest public event.

Devonport (left) and Stonehouse (below) are the settlements that grew into the present-day city of Plymouth. Originally a fishing village, Stonehouse started to develop with the completion of three military facilities: the Royal Naval Hospital in 1762, the Royal Marine barracks in 1783 and the Royal William Victualling Yard in 1835. Of the three, only the barracks are still in use today. The 16-acre Royal William Victualling Yard served as stores for food, drink and munitions for the navy. It closed in 1992, and is now undergoing a £110m regeneration including residential and office space plus leisure facilities. Near the tall blue building, ferries leave from Millbay docks bound for Roscoff in France and Santander in Spain.

PLYMOUTH

Strategically important for centuries, Plymouth is situated between the rivers Tamar and Plym, where they flow into Plymouth Sound. It was mentioned in the Domesday Book, was the first town in the country to receive its charter in 1439 and became a city in 1928. The Royal Citadel (below) on the waterfront was built in 1665 by Charles II in anticipation of a Dutch invasion. The 70ft (21m) high walls made it the country's most important fortification for over 100 years. During the 1750s, 113 guns were added. The citadel is still used today, and is open to visitors during the summer. The adjacent green space is Plymouth Hoe. Here, in 1588, Sir Francis Drake is said to have insisted on completing his game of bowls before he set sail to confront the Spanish Armada. Today you will find Drake's statue, together with the red and white Smeaton's tower, which used to guard the Eddystone Rocks nine miles (14km) offshore. The almost circular 1930s art deco Tinside pool reopened to the public in 2005 after a £3.4 million renovation.

THE BARBICAN

The area to the north and west of the former harbour of Plymouth is known as the Barbican and is steeped in history. For centuries this was home to Plymouth's fishermen and fish market. To the left of the entry lock to what is now the 467-berth Sutton Harbour Marina (pictured above) are the Mayflower Steps. The Pilgrim Fathers sailed from here in *The Mayflower* in 1620 to establish the new colony of Plymouth in modern-day Massachusetts. Also in the Barbican is the Black Friars distillery where Plymouth gin has been made since 1793. Due to its naval importance, Plymouth was heavily bombed by the Germans during the Second World War. The first bombs fell on the city on 6 July 1940 and the last of the 59 raids that became known as the Plymouth Blitz came on 30 April 1944. Much of the city centre was reduced to rubble, 1,172 civilians were killed and 4,448 injured. After the war the city centre (above left) was rebuilt according to plans drawn up by Sir Patrick Abercrombie. As a reminder of the devastation caused by the war, the ruins of Charles Church stand guard on one of the city's busy roundabouts (right). Consecrated in 1665 and the second oldest parish church in Plymouth, it was almost destroyed by incendiary bombs during the nights of 21 and 22 March 1941. A recent addition to the Plymouth skyline is the National Marine Aquarium situated across from the Mayflower Steps. Britain's largest aquarium, it opened in 1998 and features three huge tanks, including Europe's deepest, with over 4,000 marine animals ranging from seahorses to sharks.

TAVISTOCK

The market town of Tavistock (above), on the western edge of Dartmoor on the river Tavy, traces its roots back to the founding of an abbey, now ruined, in AD961. In the 14th century Tavistock was a mining town, one of Europe's largest sources of tin where the metal was weighed and stamped. Tavistock's most illustrious son, Sir Francis Drake, was born at Crowndale Farm around 1540. Drake was to become the first Englishman to circumnavigate the world, a journey which took him from 1577 until 1580. The viaduct seen in the left of the picture once carried trains on the Plymouth Devonport and South Western Junction Railway; it opened in 1890. Today it is part of the national cycle network's route 27. At the annual Tavistock food festival growers from Cornwall, Devon, Dorset and Somerset promote and sell their quality produce.

KING'S TOR

One of the many of Dartmoor's famous tors, the 1314ft (400m) high King's Tor (right) lies to the south-east of Merrivale. It is encircled by the Dartmoor Way foot and cycle path.

Close to the confluence of the rivers Tavy and Tamar, the Tavy railway bridge (left) carries the line from Plymouth over the river to Calstock.

DARTMOOR PRISON

High up on the moor, Dartmoor Prison (left and above) dominates the village of Princetown. It was built between 1806 and 1809. The first occupants were French and American prisoners of war, from the Napoleonic Wars and the War of 1812 respectively. Owned by the Duchy of Cornwall, the prison is now a category C establishment. It won the Most Improved Prison award in 2005. In the annual Dartmoor Jailbreak, a charity event, teams of two or more people – not inmates – in prison uniform compete for the furthest distance travelled without paying for their transport. The record so far is New Zealand!

DARTMEET

The woody setting of Dartmeet (right) in the heart of Dartmoor is well named: it is the meeting point of the East and West Dart rivers. From here the river Dart flows down off the moor south-eastwards through Buckfastleigh and Totnes before reaching the sea beyond Dartmouth. Beside an ancient, partially collapsed clapper bridge, a more substantial twin-arched bridge carries the road over the East Dart. Upstream is the Badger's Holt tearoom, said to be "the most famous tearoom on Dartmoor", which offers Devon cream teas prepared to a secret 50-year-old recipe.

DARTMOOR

Created in 1951, Dartmoor National Park is one of the country's last remaining wildernesses. It covers an area of 368 square miles and is rich in wildlife and archaeological remains. The highest point on the moor is at High Willhays, 2040ft (621m) above sea level. More than half of the national park is private land, owned by such bodies as the Duchy of Cornwall and the Ministry of Defence. Since 1985 walkers have been free to roam where they wish and the moor's 450 miles (720km) of bridleways and paths are for guidance only. Over 29,000 people live within Dartmoor, which is also home to the native Dartmoor pony. These ponies are all owned by local farmers, who mark them either by tagging or cutting their tail hair in a distinctive way. A particular feature of Dartmoor are its exposed and windswept tors, large hills usually topped with rocky outcrops. There are over 160 tors, the best known of which is Hay Tor (above and left) at 1500ft (457m). Stone from the nearby granite quarries was used to build the first London Bridge in 1831. Close by is Hound Tor (below left), another fine example.

At the beginning of May, thousands of 14- to 20-year-olds, in teams of six, gather at the army base at Okehampton to embark on the annual Ten Tors Challenge. Over 24 hours they must visit 10 tors on a set route, carrying all their supplies and equipment with them. Arduous terrain and frequent high winds and driving rain make this quite a challenge.

GRIMSPOUND

Just below Hameldown Tor in the north-west of Dartmoor lie the late Bronze Age remains of Grimspound (left and below). It is a massive granite wall surrounding 24 hut circles, thought to have been settled around 1300BC. One hut still features a doorway with two stone uprights. Reverend Richard Polwhele first named the settlement Grimspound in his 1797 book *History of Devon*. The name possibly derives from Grim, the Anglo-Saxon god of war, more widely known as Odin.

Uncle Tom Cobley and all came to Widecombe Fair, according to the 1880 folk song. The annual agricultural fair at Widecombe-in-the-Moor (left) continues on the second Tuesday in September, with maypole dancing and bale tossing. The 120ft (37m) tower of St Pancras church, known as the Cathedral of the Moors, can be seen from afar.

There has been an abbey at Buckfast (right) since 1018. The first monks were Benedictines: 343 years after the Dissolution of the Monasteries in 1539 they returned in 1882. Today the abbey is renowned for its honey and its colony of honeybees, and also for its tonic wine – the development of which is attributed to French monks who settled at the abbey in the 1880s.

BURGH ISLAND

Just 656ft (200m) offshore from Bigbury-on-Sea sits Burgh Island
(above). The island's buildings include the Pilchard Inn pub and
the art deco Burgh Island Hotel, dating from 1929. At low tide
visitors can walk to the island; at other times the hotel operates a
sea-tractor service, seen right in mid-crossing. The first sea-tractor
was built in 1930 and today's vehicle dates from 1969. The driver and
passengers sit on an elevated platform, whilst the Fordson tractor
powered wheelbase crosses the sand underwater. During the
Second World War wounded RAF personnel would come to
Burgh Island Hotel to convalesce. Agatha Christie visited the
island and used it as the setting for two of her books.

BANTHAM AND THURLESTONE

The sandy beaches at Bantham (left) and Thurlestone are some of the best on the South Devon coast and the Blue Flag Bantham beach has excellent surfing and windsurfing. The village of Bantham itself lies upstream from the coast, on the banks of the unspoilt river Avon. Thurlestone takes its name from an arch-shaped rock, or "thirled stone", just offshore in the bay (shown bottom left below). The village's two beaches are separated by the Thurlestone golf course; its third hole is played out on Warren Point.

KINGSBRIDGE AND THE KINGSBRIDGE ESTUARY

The market town of Kingsbridge lies at the northern end of the Kingsbridge estuary, six miles (10km) from the sea. The estuary (below), noted for its creeks and side channels, is situated in the South Devon area of outstanding natural beauty. Kingsbridge derives its name from a 10th century bridge linking the royal estates of Alvington and Chillington. The Abbot of Buckfast was granted permission for a market here in 1219. The monks sold honey, cream and scones and this market tradition, including a farmers' market, continues every Tuesday and Saturday. The town centre (right) features several 18th and 19th century buildings including the Shambles market arcade. Running off Fore Street are intriguingly named passages such as Western Backway and Squeeze Belly Alley.

SALCOMBE

Close to the mouth of the Kingsbridge estuary, Salcombe (right and below right) has a proud tradition as a boatbuilding and seafaring port. Several ships lie wrecked in the surrounding waters including a Bronze Age ship, one of only three known in the country. By the 19th century Salcombe had become an important centre for the fruit trade and the local boatyards were busy producing the Salcombe schooner. These fast vessels brought oranges and lemons from the Azores and pineapples from the Bahamas. However the boatyards found themselves unable to compete with the iron and steel craft of the northern and Scottish shipyards, so they reverted to producing fishing and sailing boats, which they continue to do. Because of its popularity amongst the sailing fraternity, property prices in Salcombe are the second-highest outside central London, after those of Sandbanks in Dorset.

START BAY

Start Point (above) juts almost claw-like about a mile out into the sea at the southern end of Start Bay, which in turn extends northwards round the coast to the Dart estuary. It is one of the most exposed peninsulas in the country. To warn of the dangers to shipping, a lighthouse was built in 1836 high on the headland, almost at the cliff edge. Designed by James Walker, it features a notable battlemented parapet. Almost at the end of the cliffs in the picture above lies the deserted village of Hallsands. Little is known of the early history of the village; by 1891 it had 37 houses. In 1900 heavy storms washed away the sea wall and 16 years later further gales and high tides broke through the village's sea defences, leaving only one property habitable. To the north of the rocks of Tinsey Head sits the fishing village of Beesands (right), known today for its lobster and crab fishing.

94

TORCROSS

Continuing around Start Bay, you reach the village of Torcross (above and inset), on the shores of the south-west's largest freshwater lake, Slapton Ley. Only the shingle beach of Slapton Sands separates this national nature reserve from the sea. In 1943 Torcross was used by 15,000 allied troops as a practice ground for the Normandy landings. But tragedy struck on 28 April 1944 when German submarines intercepted a convoy of ships taking part in these D-Day rehearsals, sinking two tank landing ships with the loss of 749 American lives.

At the northern end of the bay lies the inviting beach of Blackpool Sands (right).

DARTMOUTH AND KINGSWEAR

The town of Dartmouth (left) lies on the west bank of the Dart estuary. The port was the point of departure for the Crusades in 1147 and 1190 and since the 14th century it has been one of the homes of the English navy. The narrow Dart estuary is guarded by two castles. Set on a rocky promontory, Dartmouth castle (far left) started life in 1388 as a coastal fort. Henry VIII added gun platforms during the 16th century. The tower of the adjacent St Petroc's church overlooks the castle, now owned by English Heritage. Naval officer training in Dartmouth goes back to 1863 when two vessels were moored on the river. The Royal Naval College (below), designed by Sir Aston Webb, was built in 1905 and overlooks the town. It is now the UK's only naval college. Former royal cadets include George V and VI, the Duke of Edinburgh, Prince Charles and the Duke of York. On the opposite bank of the Dart estuary lies the village of Kingswear (bottom left). It is connected to Dartmouth by three ferries, a passenger ferry and two vehicle ferries, one known as the Dartmouth-Kingswear floating bridge, which allows traffic on the A379 road to bypass the town centre. Kingswear was the final stop on the Dartmouth and Torbay Railway, which opened in 1864 and became part of the Great Western Railway in 1876. The line faced closure in 1968 and was purchased in 1972 by the Dart Valley Railway Company. Today it is promoted as the Paignton and Dartmouth Steam Railway attracting holidaymakers and railway buffs. Opposition from local seamen and merchants meant that the station that was built at Dartmouth never saw a train and the station building is today a café.

TOTNES

Totnes is located at the highest navigable point and the lowest bridging point at
the head of the Dart estuary. It can trace its roots back to 907 when its first castle
was built by the Breton, Juhel of Totnes. By the 12th century Totnes was an
important market town and remains so today. Regular markets are held every
Friday and Saturday in the town's square, bordered by the L-shaped green roofed
Civic Hall building (above). The town's many impressive buildings include a
number of Elizabethan merchant's houses and the Eastgate, which spans the High
Street. Totnes is on the main London to Penzance railway line, but it was also on
the Buckfastleigh, Totnes and South Devon Railway which opened in 1872. A
casualty of the Beeching cuts in the 1960s, the line reopened as the Dart Valley
Railway in 1969 with steam trains once again running between Totnes and
Buckfastleigh. Renamed the South Devon Railway, the line was acclaimed
Heritage Railway of the Year 2007. As part of the Transition Towns movement, in
March 2007 Totnes was the first UK town to introduce its own local currency, the
Totnes pound. This was an effort to boost the local economy but in a sustainable
manner. About 70 businesses in the town now accept this alternative currency.

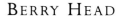

BERRY HEAD

This limestone peninsula forms the southern extremity of Torbay and rises 200ft (65m) above the sea. With a mild climate and exposed situation, Berry Head (left) is one of Britain's 200 national nature reserves. Its thin soil is home to rare plants including the goldilocks aster, early gentian and white rockrose. The surrounding cliffs boast colonies of guillemots, black-legged kittiwakes and razorbills; below, the caves house a colony of endangered greater horseshoe bats. The headland is guarded by Napoleonic fortifications, built between 1795 and 1806. At the other end sits the Berry Head lighthouse (below left), the smallest, highest and deepest lighthouse in the British Isles. It dates from 1906 and is just 16ft (5m) high, but sits 190ft (58m) above the mean high water line. The adjacent cliff sides of the former Berry Head quarry are popular with aficionados of deep-water soloing, an extreme sport, where climbers forgo ropes and let the water cushion any fall. Berry Head House, now a hotel, used to be the home of Reverend Henry Francis Lyte. When he was close to death in 1847, he was inspired by the view over the bay to write the moving words of the hymn *Abide with Me*.

BRIXHAM

The busy fishing port and town of Brixham (above) lies at the southern end of Torbay. It featured as *Briseham* in the Domesday Book, with a population of just 39. In the town centre today stands a statue of William of Orange, later William III of England, who landed here on November 5 1688 with an army of 20,000 men and 5,000 horses. Many locals have Dutch surnames, a sign that they are descendants of soldiers in his army. Brixham is said to be the "mother of deep-sea fisheries" as its boats helped develop such ports as Hull and Grimsby and today it has a small fleet of vintage restored vessels that can be seen in the picture left. The port is still one of the country's most important in the value of the fish landed. The fish market (left) is open to the public on two days during the summer when you can learn more about catching and cooking fish. Brixham marina can accommodate up to 500 craft. Between the marina and the outer harbour breakwater the orange Torbay lifeboat can be seen. The Torbay lifeboat station, based in Brixham since 1866, is one of the busiest in the country with about 100 launches per year. The circular wake visible in the picture, near the fish market, was created by a 138-seater catamaran. For a four-week trial period in August 2008 it operated a fast-ferry service between Brixham and Torquay. By road this journey can take over 40 minutes, often longer in the high season; by sea the crossing is just 15 minutes.

TORQUAY

Torquay (above), at the northern end of Torbay, boasts over 500 hotels and more Blue Flag beaches than any other UK resort. The distinctive cabbage trees (*cordyline australis*), which give the town a Mediterranean feel, were introduced from New Zealand in 1820 and have thrived in the mild climate and long hours of sunshine. The town started its life as a holiday resort in the 19th century. The first visitors were the families of officers in the Royal Navy whose ships were anchored in the bay during the Napoleonic wars. In the First World War survivors of the Battle of Gallipoli recuperated in military hospitals, and during the Second World War evacuees arrived from London. Over 23,000 US troops left Torquay for Utah Beach in Normandy in the D-Day landings in 1944. Four years later, Torquay staged the aquatic events of the London Olympics. Torquay is the birthplace of the crime novelist Agatha Christie and the writer and comedian Peter Cook. John Cleese is said to have been inspired by life at the Gleneagles Hotel for his classic sitcom *Fawlty Towers*. On Beacon Quay (right) sits Torquay's newest attraction. Opened in 2004 and part of Paignton zoo, Living Coasts boasts various marine animals and sea birds.

DAWLISH WARREN

The sandy spit that is Dawlish Warren (below right) stretches for two miles (3km) out into the mouth of the Exe estuary. The long sandy beach is popular with families and is backed by an 18-hole golf course and a nature reserve. The 500-acre reserve boasts over 450 different plant species, including the unique Warren crocus, which is protected by Act of Parliament. The neighbouring dunes are home to a large numbers of birds, both indigenous and migratory. The railway line from Exeter to Paignton is promoted as the Riviera Line. It follows the Exe estuary and then cuts behind Langstone Rock (pictured right) before hugging the coast beyond Dawlish Warren to Teignmouth. Visitors to Dawlish Warren have a choice of accommodation ranging from holiday parks and campsites to staying in one of eight converted railway carriages with all mod cons.

EXETER

The county town of Devon, Exeter's roots are probably Celtic in origin. The Celts gave way to the Romans, who founded their city of *Isca Dumnoniorum* on the banks of the Exe in AD50. The city was at the southern end of the Fosse Way Roman road and parts of the Roman walls can still be seen today. Pride of place in the city centre goes to Exeter's Anglican cathedral, dedicated to St Peter (shown centre above). It was founded in 1050 when the episcopal seat was moved from Crediton to Exeter. The first Bishop of Exeter, Leofric, was personally installed by Edward the Confessor. The building we see today dates from 1400 and boasts the longest vaulted ceiling in the country. Early in Exeter's history, the tidal river Exe was navigable right up to the city walls and it was a busy port. But over the centuries weirs were built in the river to control its flow, and trade was threatened. This was resolved by building the canal, completed in 1567 and featuring the country's first pound locks. Miller's Crossing bridge, a new pedestrian and cycle bridge (shown bottom right), opened in 2002.

CITY CENTRE

With the arrival of the railways in 1844, Exeter continued to thrive and grow as a trading centre. Today the city's two mainline stations, Exeter St David's and Exeter Central, link it not only to London and Plymouth but also to Bristol, Birmingham and the North. Exeter suffered 18 German bombing raids during the Second World War and much of the city centre was flattened. The cathedral also received a direct hit but has been fully restored. In the 1950s the area between the cathedral and the High Street was developed and became the Princesshay pedestrian shopping precinct, the first of its kind in the country. A £200m redevelopment in 2007 has resulted in Princesshay's revival as a more modern shopping centre (right). In addition to three major stores and 60 other shops, along with cafés and restaurants, the new development also includes 123 one- and two-bedroom apartments. In 2004 Exeter became a Fair-trade City. Today Exeter's three largest employers are the university, Devon County Council and the Meteorological Office or Met Office, the UK's weather forecasting service, which moved from Bracknell in 2004. The Met Office college trains national forecasters and also those from overseas.

EXMOUTH AND BUDLEIGH SALTERTON

Exmouth (right), is an attractive holiday resort by the sea at the mouth of the river Exe. With its varied architecture and location the town gained popularity when the railway arrived in 1861. The marina was converted from the old docks in 2002. Orcombe Point in Exmouth is the starting point for the Jurassic Coast, a World Heritage Site stretching for 95 miles (153km) to Old Harry Rocks in Dorset.

The elderly residents of Budleigh Salterton (below) give the resort a genteel air. Red Devonian sandstone cliffs bookend the town's pebble beach which runs for 2¹⁄₂ miles (4km) to the mouth of the river Otter at Otterhead. A short distance to the north of Budleigh is Hayes Barton, birthplace of Walter Raleigh. Sir John Everett Millais captured a moment in Raleigh's childhood in his painting *The Boyhood of Raleigh*, which hangs at Tate Britain in London.

SIDMOUTH

Sidmouth (above) featured in the Domesday Book as the fishing village of *Sedmuda*. It developed into a fashionable holiday resort in the 18th and 19th centuries. Today the fine Georgian and Regency villas on the promenade are hotels. At the western edge of the town, the pebble beach gives way to sand at Jacob's Ladder, which is accessed from the clifftop gardens by a steep wooden staircase. The town's folk festival, held every August, has grown in scope and reputation: from lowly beginnings in 1955 it has become the Sidmouth International Folklore Festival. To the east of the town rises the mighty Salcombe Hill Cliff (right). A red Devon sandstone cliff, it dates from the Triassic period and is characteristic of the cliffs on this section of the World Heritage Jurassic Coast. To the west, in Ladrum Bay, there are several offshore stacks, such as Big Picket Rock (left) which rises 140ft (43m).

BEER

The unspoilt fishing village of Beer (above and right) was once surrounded by forests, and takes its name from the Anglo-Saxon word *bere* or *beare* meaning woodland. It is sheltered from the prevailing winds by Beer Head and the high cliffs nearby. The village thrived on fishing and smuggling. Jack Rattenbury, Devon's most notorious smuggler, was born in Beer in 1778 and visitors can still see the caves where contraband goods were stored. All fishing boats have to be hauled up on to the beach as there is no harbour. Twenty-four of Britain's cathedrals and famous buildings have used stone quarried in Beer; they include Exeter cathedral, St Paul's, the Tower of London and Windsor castle. Stone has been quarried here since Roman times. At Pecorama, above Beer, young and old can enjoy a ride on the Beer Heights light railway, which opened in 1975.

SEATON

At the mouth of the river Axe lies Seaton (right and below), an attractive holiday resort set between white limestone and red sandstone cliffs. While the town's roots date back to before the Romans, it was first known as Seaton in 1146. Until the 14th century, when a landslide partly blocked the estuary, the town was an important port. The harbour further declined with the arrival of the railway in 1868. A victim of the Beeching cuts in the 1960s, the railway line was acquired by Claude Lane and converted to a tramway. The Seaton Tramway made its first journey up the Axe valley to Colyton on 28 August 1970 and today it carries over 100,000 passengers a year. Next to the tramway lies the newly established Seaton Marshes local nature reserve, particularly known as a place to see a large number of wading birds in winter and butterflies and dragonflies in summer.

DORSET

While not the largest county in England, Dorset can certainly claim to be one of the richest both scenically and historically. Its 87 miles (140km) of World Heritage coastline contains some of the country's best examples of geological phenomena: a tombolo, a natural rock arch, a limestone island and a cove. Such is the quality of its inshore waters that Olympic and Paralympic sailors will be converging on Dorset during the 2012 London Games. Set in the rolling countryside of the interior lie more of Dorset's jewels: timeless hillside carvings, busy market towns and villages and lush river valleys. Over the centuries, Dorset has been favoured by the Romans, by the royals and by the literary great – including Thomas Hardy, whose novels were inspired by country life in Dorset in the 19th century.

JURASSIC COAST

The Triassic, Jurassic and Cretaceous rock formations of the Jurassic Coast encapsulate 185 million years of the Earth's history. This 95-mile (153km) coastline was designated a UNESCO World Heritage Site in 2001. Landslips frequently expose Jurassic fossils on the section of beach known as the Undercliff (above), by Lyme Regis. One of Britain's three shingle structures, Chesil Beach (right) stretches for 18 miles (29km) and supposedly consists of 180 billion pebbles!

LYME REGIS

The "Pearl of Dorset", Lyme Regis (left and right) sits just on the Devon/Dorset border overlooking Lyme Bay. Lyme was mentioned in the Domesday Book; when it received its royal charter in 1284, Regis was added to the town's name. Between the 16th and 18th centuries the harbour was a centre of trade with France. The protective harbour wall, which is known as the Cobb, features prominently in Jane Austen's 1818 novel *Persuasion*. A century and a half later local author John Fowles based *The French Lieutenant's Woman* here.

The cliffs near Lyme are rich in fossils. The town holds an annual Mary Anning Day in memory of the famous 19th century fossil-collector, and every May it stages the Lyme Regis fossil festival.

CHARMOUTH

Jane Austen visited Lyme Regis three times at the beginning of the 19th century and described Charmouth (left) as a "sweet retired bay, backed with dark cliffs, where fragments of low rock among the sands make it the happiest spot for watching the flow of the tide". The village lies at the mouth of the river Char and is also popular with fossil-hunters. A large ammonite about 3ft (1m) in diameter can be seen in a rock under Church cliffs. To the east of the village is Golden Gap, a hill and cliff that, at 626ft (191m), is the highest point on the south coast. Golden Gap takes its name from a distinctive triangle of golden Greensand rock near its summit.

BRIDPORT

A mile and a half (2km) from the sea, where the rivers Brit and Asker meet, is the market town of Bridport (left). Saxon in origin, Bridport became a town and a centre for rope-making in the 12th century. A characteristic of the town are its wide streets across which the ropes were spun. Ropes are still made here today, using artificial fibres.

The harbour at West Bay (above) can trace its roots back to the 13th century when it was known as Bridport Mouth. When the Great Western Railway extended the line to the harbour in 1884 they adopted the name West Bay to attract holidaymakers. Every August a torchlight procession with 1,500 torches winds its way from Bridport to West Bay as part of the Bridport carnival.

ABBOTSBURY SWANNERY

Swans have been raised at Abbotsbury (right) since the 1040s when Benedictine monks established a monastery here. At the Dissolution of the Monasteries in 1539 the area was purchased by the Strangways family, whose descendants still own it. The swannery is unique – it is the only managed colony of mute swans in the world today.

CHESIL BEACH

The largest landform of its type in Britain, Chesil Beach (right) is said to be made up of 180bn pebbles that range from pea-sized near West Bay to fist-sized near Portland. It is, on average, 175 yards (160m) wide and 39ft (12m) high. For eight miles (13km) of its 18-mile (29km) length Chesil Beach is separated from the mainland by the salty water of the Fleet Lagoon. These waters were used as a practice ground for what became known as the Dambusters' raid over Germany in the Second World War. Today, this site of special scientific interest attracts many species of wildfowl.

THE ISLE OF PORTLAND

The limestone mass of Portland measures four and a half miles
(7km) by one and three quarter miles (3km). A Royal Manor, it is
joined to the mainland by Chesil Beach. The Portland stone that is
quarried here is renowned all over the world: it was used for the
Cenotaph in Whitehall and more than half a million Portland
stone gravestones were shipped to France and Belgium for their
vast war cemeteries. It was also used in London's Buckingham
Palace and St Paul's cathedral, as well as the United Nations
building in New York.

Portland harbour (above and right) is the one of the deepest, and
largest, man-made harbours in the world. Prisoners – there are two
prisons on Portland today – were used to quarry the stone for the
huge breakwaters, completed in 1872. Until it closed in 1995,
Portland harbour was one of Britain's main naval bases. Pride of
place in the harbour now goes to the Weymouth and Portland
National Sailing Academy which opened in 2000. The sailing events
at the 2012 Olympic and Paralympic games will be staged here.

Since 1716 the lighthouse at Portland Bill (above right) has warned
shipping of the strong currents that make the waters off Portland
so hazardous.

WEYMOUTH

With the natural advantage of a third more hours of sunshine than the rest of the country, it is no surprise that Weymouth developed as one of England's first holiday resorts. George III visited 14 times between 1789 and 1805, and the elegant Georgian and Regency buildings that line the esplanade bear witness to Weymouth's growth during this period. A century earlier, between 1702-05, Sir Christopher Wren had been the town's MP. He controlled the quarries at Portland and used Portland stone for many of his buildings. Nothe Fort (left) was built to protect Portland's harbour in 1872; today it is a museum devoted to the Second World War.

Outside the peak season, the town's wide sandy beach hosts various sporting events. The international beach kite-flying festival in May regularly attracts over 40,000 spectators. Beyond the marina, in the centre of the town (above) is Radipole Lake, an important RSPB nature reserve and habitat for reedbed birds. With well laid-out trails and activities for children, it is ideal for a family visit.

Local people still think of Weymouth station (right) as Weymouth Town station, to distinguish it from Weymouth Quay station, now the Condor Ferries terminal. Their fast ferries operate to the Channel Islands and to St Malo in France.

OSMINGTON WHITE HORSE

The figure of King George III astride a horse is carved into the hill near Sutton Poyntz and is visible from Weymouth and Portland. It is 323ft (98m) high and 280ft (85m) wide; its tail is as wide as a street. Dating from 1807, the figure faces away from the town. Locals still debate whether it shows the king's alleged displeasure with Weymouth or him simply going east to call on Sir Thomas Weld, the owner of nearby Lulworth Castle.

AXE VALLEY

The river Axe meanders gently from its source near Beaminster in north Dorset down to the sea near Seaton in east Devon. Flowing through rich agricultural land the Axe shows no particular allegiance to any one county: along its course it forms part of both the Dorset/Somerset and the Devon/Dorset borders. Only 22 miles (35km) long, the river is quite shallow and popular with anglers who come to fish its river and sea trout and the occasional salmon. The River Axe Walk enables ramblers to enjoy the valley's outstanding beauty and architectural gems such as Forde Abbey, on the Dorset side of the river. The abbey was founded as a Cistercian monastery in 1148 and became a great seat of learning. Edmund Prideaux, the MP for Lyme Regis, bought the former abbey in 1649 and set about creating a splendid family home, which it remains today. In 2008 Forde Abbey and Gardens won the silver award in the small visitor attraction class in Enjoy England's Award for Excellence competition.

DORCHESTER

Dorchester (right and below) is the county town of Dorset. As a large Iron Age hill fort it was one of the most important settlements in pre-Roman Britain. By AD70 the Romans had named the town *Durnovaria*. The Roman remains in the town today include Maumbury Rings, which was used as an amphitheatre.

In 1832 a group of labourers formed the Friendly Society of Agricultural Labourers. As trades unions were illegal at that time they were arrested and tried in Dorchester's Shire Hall. These men became known as the Tolpuddle Martyrs and were sentenced to transportation to Australia.

The centre of Dorchester (right) remains compact and features several interesting buildings from the 17th to 19th centuries including the Town Hall and King's Arms and Borough Arms Pubs. On the western edge of the town development is taking place at Poundbury on land owned by the Duchy of Cornwall. The design of the estate echoes the street pattern of the centre of the town and is guided by the Prince of Wales' commitment to traditional architecture. When complete, Poundbury will consist of 2,500 houses and be home to about 6,000 people.

SHAFTESBURY

Overlooking the beautiful Blackmore Vale, Shaftesbury is the only hilltop town of
any significance in Dorset. At 750ft (250m) above sea level it is one of Britain's
highest towns – and one of the oldest. Its roots date back to 880 when it was
founded by King Alfred. Only ruins remain of Shaftesbury Abbey, which Alfred
had built and where he installed his daughter as the first prioress. The abbey was
to become the richest nunnery in England but was destroyed in 1539 on the
orders of Thomas Cromwell.

Shaftesbury features as *Shaston* in the Thomas Hardy novels *Tess of the
d'Urbervilles* and *Jude the Obscure*, which were published in 1891 and 1895. More
recently, the town's Gold Hill starred in the 1973 television advertisement for
Hovis bread, directed by Ridley Scott. To the music of Dvorak's Ninth Symphony,
a young boy is seen pushing his bicycle up the one-in-four cobbled hill. The
advert ran throughout the 1970s and 1980s and Gold Hill, with its 18th century
cottages, became one of the most familiar streets in the country. It was screened
again in May 2006 to celebrate the company's 120th anniversary. The churchyard of
Holy Trinity church (right) boasts three fine avenues of lime trees. The church
dates from 1842 and has been converted for use by the community.

CERNE ABBAS GIANT

The earliest written mention of the Cerne Abbas giant (right) dates from 1694, but its origin is unknown. Also known as the Rude Man (meaning naked man), the giant is cut into a steep chalk hill north of Dorchester. At 180ft (55m) tall and 167ft (51m) wide, with a 120ft (37m) long knobbly club, he is best seen from across the valley or from the air. The National Trust now owns the site, which is grazed by local sheep. In 2008 extra manpower (seen here) was required to give the giant a makeover, applying 17 tonnes of chalk.

DURDLE DOOR

The dramatic natural arch at Durdle Door (above and right) is the most photographed spot on the Jurassic Coast. The name evolved from the Old English word *thirl*, meaning to pierce.

The limestone arch was formed by the erosion of softer rocks over thousands of years. The arch sits at one end of a T-shaped isthmus that rises to a height of 400ft (120m) above the sea near Lulworth. Geologists expect that the top of the arch will eventually fall into the sea, and leave a stone stack similar to those at Ladram Bay in Devon.

Durdle Door has been filmed as a backdrop to pop music videos for artists including Cliff Richard and Tears for Fears. It has also starred in a number of films including the 1997 film *Wilde* with Stephen Fry and the 2005 children's film *Nanny McPhee* adapted by the actress Emma Thompson.

124

LULWORTH COVE

Over one million people visit Lulworth Cove every year. The shell-shaped cove was formed some 10,000 years ago as a result of erosion by glacial melt water and wave action. Behind the narrow Portland limestone entrance, the process continues with the softer Purbeck limestone, Wealdon clay, Greensand sandstone and chalk being eroded still. The pebble beach is naturally very sheltered. Nearly half a mile (800m) to the east is Stair Hole, which as an infant cove gives the visitor an idea of what Lulworth Cove might have looked liked as it evolved. The sea has breached the Portland and Purbeck limestone here and also made a small arch.

Many fossils have been found in and around Lulworth Cove and the area has interested geologists and geographers since the beginning of the 19th century. The first major study was carried out in the 1830s and geology students still flock here from all over the world. Lulworth's very own butterfly, the Lulworth Skipper (*thymelicus acteon*) was discovered in 1832. The butterfly was first spotted near Durdle Door and is rarely found more than five miles from the sea on the south coast.

125

CHAPMAN'S POOL AND DURLSTON HEAD

The easiest way to explore Chapman's Pool (above) is by boat: just anchor in the bay and row ashore. To reach this idyllic spot on foot you have to climb 400ft (122m) down a precarious path to the water's edge where there are a few fishermen's huts.

The lower of the three points (right) is Durlston Head, the others are Peveril Point and the Foreland. Durlston Head, now a country park, offers an ideal habitat for a wide range of animals and birds. The cliffs here form the southern limit of the Isle of Purbeck and provide a perfect place for dolphin watching. Situated within the country park and just two miles from Swanage, Anvil Point lighthouse (foreground) was opened in 1881.

SWANAGE AND FORELAND POINT

Swanage (left) became a holiday resort at the beginning of the 19th century when the local MP converted one of the town's mansions into a luxury hotel. Princess Victoria, later queen, stayed at the hotel in 1833, when it was renamed the Royal Victoria Hotel. The hotel is no more but visitors still come to Swanage to enjoy the town's pier and the sandy beach that stretches around the bay.

The railway reached Swanage in 1885. British Rail closed the line in 1972, removing all the track. Local enthusiasts subsequently formed the Swanage Railway Society in 1975 and gradually set about rebuilding the line. Today volunteers operate steam and diesel trains between Swanage and Norden, a distance of six miles (10km).

The Foreland or Handfast Point (below) separates Swanage Bay from Studland Bay. At the end of the chalk point the Old Harry Rocks form a fine finale to the Jurassic Coast.